Francis Pott

An introduction to the principles and practice of chanting in

free rhythm and true antiphony as embodied in the

Free-rhythm psalter

Francis Pott

An introduction to the principles and practice of chanting in free rhythm and true antiphony as embodied in the Free-rhythm psalter

ISBN/EAN: 9783337276546

Printed in Europe, USA, Canada, Australia, Japan

Cover: Foto ©Thomas Meinert / pixelio.de

More available books at **www.hansebooks.com**

INTRODUCTION [1]

PART I.

'Vox ancilla verbi.'

A NEW pointed Psalter may justly be challenged to justify
its claims in the face of more than a score of predecessors,
Anglican and Gregorian. But it is this very multitude of com-
petitors which is its first and best justification. For every fresh
Psalter has been a witness to the failure of all before it to
satisfy some considerable number of people. Of course, some
new Psalters, accompanied with chants, are partly due to a
desire for better chants, or better choice and assignment of
chants; but all alike set themselves to amend the pointing.
This failure of all existing pointing is further shown by the
warm controversy still kept up between the two 'systems'
under which they are all now classified, the so-called 'Cathedral'
system, and the so-called 'Church' system; though they are
not really two systems, but one system applied in different
degrees.

It would surprise the reader, if I could quote here from
letters sent unsought to myself alone, and therefore repre-
senting a much more widely spread dissatisfaction with our
Anglican chanting, the many plaintive appeals for some reform,
or vigorous condemnations of the methods now most prevalent,
from experienced Organists, Choirmasters, and Clergy. But
the fact of this general dissatisfaction is also shown, and at the
same time its unrecognized cause is revealed, by the frequent
use of such expressions of dislike as 'choppy chanting,' 'rigid,'
'cut and dried, chants,' and by complaints that the Psalms are

---

[1] Much of Parts I and II of this Introduction appeared in substance
in *The Organist and Choirmaster*, of January and February 1895, where
it gave rise to much interesting discussion, of which advantage has
been gratefully taken in its revision and enlargement.

B

made to move 'in fetters,' or 'in a strait waistcoat,' or drilled, against nature, to keep step with the measured tread of metrical music ; and by protests on behalf of the solemn tone and stately rhythm of the Psalms, against the undignified 'jingle' of many Anglican chants.

The secret of their failure is to be found in the point from which all existing pointed Psalters start, viz., that, the chant being what it is, the words of the Psalms must be made to conform to it. 'The Anglican chant is a *fact*,' they say, and 'it is a melody of seven (or five) bars'; in other words, it is a metrical tune, like a hymn tune, except as regards the reciting note ; and some deny even this exception.

But there is nothing sacred about an Anglican chant. If it comes into collision with another fact stronger and more unalterable than itself, it must either conform thereto, or make way for something else ; and that other fact is this ;—that the Psalms and Canticles are *non-metrical* ; they are in what is called *free rhythm*, or rhythmic prose, the grandest form of poetry, but *not* in metre. And they and their poetic form *are* sacred and unalterable, except with a violence which *is* sacrilege. It is the hitherto constant struggle between the tyranny of the rigid metrical chant, and the free-born, but fettered, Psalm rhythm, that has caused, without being generally detected, the dissatisfaction and murmuring about Anglican chanting. And the remedy must be found in a different conception from that commonly entertained as to the true nature and form of the Chant, and its relation to that of the Psalm ; this Psalter is not, therefore, merely one more endeavour to repoint the Psalms, i. e. to improve the usual pointing in particular passages ; it is an attempt to reconsider the matter afresh ; to go back to first principles, to historical precedents, and to early English examples.

It is not necessary, of course, to insist upon the first principle of all,—that church music is wholly for the glory of God and the help of man in worshipping Him ; it is enough to begin with the principle embodied in our motto, 'Vox ancilla verbi,' —'Music the handmaid, not the mistress, of the words'; and to remember that, as far as chanting is concerned, the words are not only fixed for us by the Church, but consecrated, in their form as well as their spirit, as part of Holy Writ. And the true question is, and should always have been, not how to make the Psalm-verse fit the form of a chant, but *how to make the chant serve the rhythm of the Psalm-verse.*

In attempting to carry out these principles four leading points have been kept in view.

Leading purposes.

FIRST. To recover a greater freedom from metrical bonds to the Rhythm of the Psalm, and more elasticity and variety of form to the Chant.

> I must here at once acknowledge my very great debt to Mr. John Heywood, whose interesting and suggestive little book on the *Art of Chanting* (Clowes) gave me the clue to the rhythmical defect in most English Chants, and to the true remedy [1].

SECONDLY. To escape the necessity, involved so constantly in the prevailing systems, of putting false emphasis on unimportant words. This second object is gained, incidentally, and yet completely, through the methods employed to obtain the first.

THIRDLY. To obtain smoothness and dignity, and to rid our chanting of the tripping, un-Psalmlike jingle of dactyls and anapaests, whether of notes or syllables. (See p. 6 III, and p. 17, note.)

FOURTHLY. To restore the true Antiphony or Responsiveness, which exists within each Psalm-verse, and within each single chant, and also within each half of a double chant,—as well as between the sides of a choir (and congregation).

To these four leading purposes everything, however unnecessary, or irrelevant, or fanciful, it may at first sight appear, is directly referable and subservient.

The Poetical Form of the Psalms.

Our first consideration must be the words of the Psalm-verse,—the form and character of their poetry.

The Psalm-verse, as distinguished from ordinary prose on one hand, and from metrical hymns on the other, has two marked characteristics of its own.

---

[1] To anticipate misapprehension it may be well to say that *absolute* freedom in concerted singing is obviously unattainable; and to add that the 'free rhythm' here spoken of has nothing in common with the 'free chant' of the late Mr. John Crowdy except a common aim. (See p. 10.)

These two characteristics are :—

(1) FREE RHYTHM ; that is to say, there is no fixed measured length of lines, no regularity in the fall of the accent, no feet, no rhyme—and yet there is a certain undefined rhythm, or well-proportioned distribution of the irregular accents, which gives them the true ring of poetic form, and a dignity far excelling that of any but the best examples of metrical verse. It is, in short, a free recitation, and primarily nothing but a recitation, with only such inflexion of voice at certain points as will give expression to its other characteristic, viz. :—

(2) ANTIPHONY or *Responsiveness*. Each verse contains in itself a verse or versicle in its first half, and a response in its last half. In order to realize this, let the reader, if he is not already aware of it, recite almost any verse, inserting 'yea' immediately after the dividing colon, or in some cases 'even,' or 'yea, even,' and if it does not interrupt, but rather develops, the sense, it obviously shows that there is this responsiveness : e. g., 'O come let us sing unto the Lord : (yea) let us heartily rejoice in the strength of our salvation.'—xcv. 1. 'O Lord, how glorious are Thy works : (yea) Thy thoughts are very deep.'—'An unwise man doth not well consider this : (yea) and a fool doth not understand it.'—xcii. 5, 6. 'The waves of the sea are mighty and rage horribly : (yea) but yet the Lord, who dwelleth on high, is mightier.'—xciii. 5. 'Because they provoked his Spirit : (even) so that he spake unadvisedly with his lips.'—'Neither destroyed they the heathen : (even) as the Lord commanded them.'—cvi. 33, 34 ; see also v. 36. It is indeed only in few instances, and in most of these because of mistakes in our Prayer Book translation or punctuation, that it will be found to fail.

To the truth of this antiphonal structure we have also a three-fold external witness, viz. (1) each verse divided into responsive halves by the colon or 'point' (see Title-page of the Book of Common Prayer), or in Latin Psalters by an asterisk ; (2) each chant divided into more or less musically responsive halves by the double bar-line ; (3) each choir divided into responsive sides, *Decani* and *Cantoris* [1].

---

[1] These characteristics of the Psalm-verse are not, indeed, confined to the 'Psalms of David,' as we call them, but are found in certain isolated Psalms or Songs in the Old Testament, e. g., his Lament over Saul and Jonathan (2 Sam. i); the two Songs of Moses ; the Songs

The result of this on the selection of Chants. These two characteristics of the Psalm-*verse* are, then, the tests of a true Psalm*chant.* No chant, no pointing, no chanting, which does not conform to these, has any claim to our acceptance.

I. **A chant therefore is by them condemned :**—*If it fail to recognize and respect the recitation as the essential and predominant element, and the rest as being merely an inflexion and close of it.* And this it fails to do—

(*a*) If it does not leave as many as possible of the words free for recitation—if, that is, the two melodies or inflexions (commonly called the Mediation and Cadence) demand so many syllables as are now generally assigned to them upon the mistaken supposition that each melody requires a strong initial accent, for which a sufficiently strong syllable cannot be found without trespassing backward upon what should be the free recitation.

(*b*) If by reason of a wide rising interval at the end of the monotone emphasizing this accent, or of a melody made prominent by other striking intervals or zigzag movements, the effect produced is that of a marked tune, starting from that accent and sharply distinct from the recitation, rather than a smooth inflected extension of it; for the recitation is thereby thrown into the shade, and becomes a mere preliminary to this tune.

(*c*) If either reciting note is out of easy reach of any ordinary voice for free natural recitation, without strain or hurry.

II. **A chant is condemned :**—*If for any reason the accent upon the last note of all is irrepressibly strong,* and so produces the awkwardly heavy accent,—the 'Anglican thump'—on the final note, which is one of the worst features of the prevailing system, leading, as it does, to an intolerable accumulation of syllables upon that note, of which we shall have to say more presently. And this is always the case in Anglican chants if the melody in the last bar but one of the chant is broken into two minims of different pitch, and cannot be written as one semibreve, so as to receive all the one concentrated accent which,—as will be presently explained,—is alone allowable in the cadence. This point is so

of Hannah and Habbakuk; the Visions of Balaam; and in the four primary Canticles of our Daily Prayer, and, with exceptions, in the Psalm *Quicunque Vult* or Athanasian Creed.

ably advocated by Mr. Heywood in his little book referred to above, that the reader cannot do better than study it there.

' III. A chant is condemned:—*If it contain anywhere in the Melody two crotchets* in the place of a minim—producing, as they always do, the undignified jingle of a dactyl or anapaest—unless they are sung as if they were minims, making, with the other minim, three minims in succession as in Tone vi, p. 10).

IV. A chant is condemned :—*If it be for any reason irreformably metrical in character.*

V. A chant is condemned :—*If it fail to represent the antiphonal character of the Psalm-verse.*

(*a*) If, for instance, there is no musical responsiveness between its Mediation and Cadence. This failure is most common in double chants; for no responsiveness between the two *pairs* of phrases, even where it exists, makes up for a failure between the Mediation and Cadence *of each pair* ; for it is there that we find the never-failing antiphony of each Psalm-verse. Unfortunately, a large number of modern chants, single and double, have been written during a period, apparently a very long period, in which the true conception of antiphony had been lost, and a mere alternating repetition of a whole chant to a whole verse (as usual in our reading of the Psalms) was substituted for it.

(*b*) And again, if the reciting notes of the two halves are so different as to produce a contrast between themselves, calculated to obscure the only desired contrast of challenge and reply in the two endings, Mediation and Cadence. The less difference between the reciting notes the truer it is to the original conception of a chant, and to the actual form of the ancient chant, as well as to the natural utterance of two presumably equal bodies in colloquy. All genuine ancient chants have the *same* reciting notes in both halves.

(*c*) And again, if the sense of expectation of a reply is lost by an undue fall at the end of the first half.

These conditions may seem so exacting as to leave but few chants available; but this is by no means the case; there is no difficulty in finding an amply sufficient number, without reckoning several expressly written to meet them. We do not want such a multitude of chants as are now in use. The continual production of new chants has begotten more than one evil. It fosters a tendency to aim at clever compositions, chromatic harmonies and enharmonic changes, which are suitable neither to the simple dignity of the words, nor to the brevity and frequent repetition of a chant. The best chants are the simplest, the smoothest, the most diatonic and transparent.

Again, we cannot but see that the unceasing supply of chants in the easy metrical form, however beautiful they may be as tunes, is a serious hindrance to the recovery of our English chanting from its unsatisfactory condition. It is estimated that there are little less than two thousand modern chants in more or less use, all claiming a sort of vested interest in the maintenance of the faulty system under which they were written. It should be remembered that a very small number of chants has sufficed for the whole of Western Christendom outside England for centuries ; the largest collection of Gregorians of all periods and localities that I know of, contains less than the number of the Psalms ; and it seems that at Saint Paul's about the end of the seventeenth century their whole repertory of chants was seventeen.

Nay, more, there is little doubt that the modern multiplication of chants has exercised a further unsuspected influence in the direction of that rigid fixity of form of which complaint is made. When chants were not more, but less, in number than the Psalms, as of old, each Psalm would naturally have some one of the chants permanently assigned to it, not perhaps universally, but locally ; and the chant, through frequent use with the Psalm, would learn to adjust its then more flexible form to the varying rhythm of each verse, and this mutual adaptation would become traditional, familiar, and, notwithstanding its variations, easy for all to follow. When, however, in England chants came to be written in considerable number, and written, not for this or that Psalm, but as independent pieces of music, it was necessary that each chant should be able, as it were, to ' stand alone,'—self contained,—with a defined and measurable form of its own ; and when *all* the chants were to be used interchangeably with *any* Psalm, it was also necessary that the form should be one and the same for all chants; and so, consequently, that every verse of every Psalm should be cut up, measured out, and made to fit this one fixed rigid form, however much its rhythm and length might resent this Procrustean treatment.

It is not, of course, to be supposed that we can now recover altogether the simplicity and flexibility of those early times, when psalms were chanted only by small bodies of monks or singing-men, and this daily to the same elastic Tones, and when there were no such difficult conditions as thoughtless volunteer choir-boys and wholly untrained congregations.

No doubt we must face some sacrifices; a sacrifice of old notions, and old habits; a sacrifice of some little trouble to overcome these, both in ourselves and others; and a sacrifice of some old favourite chant-tunes. But it by no means involves the abandonment of Anglican chants; it is indeed an effort to save all (and they are many) which either do now conform, or can be easily made to conform, to the conditions which are demanded by a true regard for the words of the Psalms; and, be it observed, any old favourites, especially double chants, can still be freely used to selections from metrical versions of the Psalms (Sternhold and Hopkins, or Tate and Brady), or to almost any of our simpler hymns, with excellent effect; and this is the true consistent use of them—*metrical chants to metrical psalms*.

It must be confessed, indeed, that there is some reason to fear that the present attempt will not be popular at first with 'the many'; it appeals rather to those who are responsible for the dignity and truthfulness of our Church's worship, and whose duty it is to lead others upward. The many as yet, one reluctantly admits, think too little of the words they sing; they like music, and such music as pleased that 'merrie Monarch,' 'that brisk and airy Prince,' Charles II, who 'liked music in Church to which he could beat time' (Hullah, from Pepys, quoted by Heywood). Neither popularity nor facility is a true and honest test of good church music, and least of all in connexion with words so sacred and so spiritual as the Psalms. And as to difficulty in practice, there is absolutely none in the method itself, but only such as must always meet us for a time while shaking ourselves free from the ideas and habits of a discarded system.

The Witness of History.

I. Antiphony.—It will be expected that what has been said should be justified by reference to the theory, origin, growth, and history of the chant. History will not carry us far back. Psalms had been chanted, as the chief element in worship by Hebrew and by Christian for 1500 years before history shows us a chant. But it is safe to assume that the germ of the chant, and its essence, was a simple recitation on one musical note (higher or lower as the character of the Psalm dictated) by two responding bodies of singers, reciting the two responsive halves of a Psalm-verse; but this in practice would immediately develop into something more. Let any two individuals (or bodies) recite on a note, antiphonally, by half-verses, a few verses of a Psalm, and they will soon crave, not only some relief from the monotone, but some very simple inflexion—rise or fall, at the end of each half-verse—to express in the first an expectation of reply, and in the second a satisfaction of that expectation by a cadence—the monotonic *recitation* still remaining the *essential part.* Now, when history at last does show us chants in the so-called Gregorian tones, it reveals to us, in the simpler and shorter forms of the 8th and other Tones, exactly this primitive pattern. But a further natural development had taken place in most of them, and the inflexion had extended backward, by two notes at least, further over the recitation: and we get nearly to the pattern, *in length,* of our Anglican chant. It will not be necessary to notice the further extension of the melody, which is found in later times in festal forms of the ancient chant.

II. Timelessness.—The original chant would be *timeless.* The primitive recitation would have, of course, no accentuation of its own, apart from that of the words, which would vary with every verse,—no measured beats, no bars, no fixed relative length of notes. When the one note of responsive inflexion was introduced at the end of each half-verse, this alone would have its accent, which would in the nature of things fall on the last *strong* syllable without any pre-arrangement or 'pointing.' When this note developed into more, still there was no regulation of their time, no fixing of their accent. No marks of time were used or known. And this is made more clear by the remarkable fact that so free, so innocent of the bonds of measured time, were the old church musicians, that they sometimes put three full notes (let us call them minims) in the space, not the time, of what we reckon a bar of common time, e. g.,

6th Tone.

And even when extending, in later times, the melody still further, in the festal forms, it is remarkable how free and irregular and unmetrical they contrived to keep them. Nay, even when they were composing melodies for *metrical* hymns, in which we hold ourselves rigidly bound to strict measure and time, they seem to have revelled in breaking away from obedience to the metre of the words, and in giving irregular numbers of notes to a foot, e. g. H. A. & M., 97, 177, 483, 486, 509; and it is a hopeless mistake of our modern editors to endeavour to divide them up into bars. This free treatment of *metrical hymns* need not be imitated in modern music; but it is of the *essence* of *chants*, which are sung to *non-metrical* words, to be *free*. And it is the fundamental and fatal want of our modern chants that they rivet the fetters of strict time upon the essentially freely-moving rhythm of the Psalms and Canticles.

There are in this Psalter *no* marks of *time, no bars*[1]; and though it is necessary to use the ordinary notation, breve, semibreve, minim, &c., these are *not* to be taken as having any *fixed* relation of length to each other; the semibreve, for instance, is longer than a minim, but not just twice as long. Measured time is the ruin of good chanting, the true characteristic of which is elasticity in accord with the free unmeasured rhythm of the words. Measured or metrical music is only suited to metre, as in hymns and metrical psalms.

The reader may be inclined to say that this free rhythm and irregular time and accent is contrary to what he has been taught of the rules of musical form, as laid down by authorities such as Professor Prout. But all those rules are merely the formulation of the facts observed in modern music, which is in almost

---

[1] Bars were not used in chants till about the middle of the last century.

all its forms metrical. The chant (including in this term the versicles and responses of our services, as well as the Psalm-chant), is an ancient and peculiar class, *sui generis*, and cannot be judged or treated by the rigid rules of measured music ; a freedom which it shares with all true recitative (see Grove's Dictionary), and with the ancient (and modern) unbarred services, such as the *Missa de Angelis* and the *Missa Regia.*

Attempts have been made to ascertain by analysis the musical *'form'* of a chant, but they can only end in a failure because they begin with a fiction. The chant is taken as 'a melody of seven bars'; but this is not a fact—except on paper. The first and fourth bars are not bars in any true sense, but unmeasurable recitative, intervening between two inflexions, isolating them and throwing them out of 'formal' relation to each other and to the whole ; while the inflexions themselves, sung to ever-varying forms of words, are *made* metrical only by forcing these words by extension or com-pression into one and ever the same form by the use of bars.

The liberation of the Psalm-verse from the tyranny of *metrical* chants is the point to be aimed at. The bondage of modern music to strict time and measure is in nothing so manifest as in this—that, whereas the musicians of old freely broke through the metre of *metrical hymns,* our modern musicians take the *prose* parts of our Prayer Book, the Creeds, the Kyrie Eleison, Sanctus, and Gloria in Excelsis, and cut them up into equal metrical feet or bars (as they do also with the Canticles) when setting them to so-called 'Services.' It is not necessary to condemn this as inadmissible ; for in these 'Services' the melody is not fixed, as in a chant, but is varied verse by verse as desired, to suit the varied rhythm of the words, and, more-over, the constraint of measured time being continuous through-out has a certain evenness and consistency of movement which tends to smoothness and dignity, though it often has an effect upon the words not unlike that upon horses constrained to keep step to music. But in chants with an unconstrained recitation, and a sudden change to a barred inflexion, the continuity is lost, and the metrical effect is intensified by the contrast.

III. Vocal unison and harmony.—But, it will be said, 'You cannot help having measured time with vocal harmonies ; you cannot without it keep the parts together.' Perhaps this is in a measure true, except with highly trained choirs and daily service. But supposing it to be so, is *vocal* harmony so absolutely necessary for *all* parts of church worship, as to rightly override a due regard for the true form and rhythm of the words? Especially is it necessary for chanting? One cannot wonder that there is an evidently growing tendency towards unisonous chanting with organ harmonies. The great authority of Dr. Hopkins, and of Dr. E. G. Monk and Sir F. A. G. Ouseley, who have published collections of chants expressly for use in this way, and the advocacy of several other experienced organists and choirmasters, all point in this direction. And it may well be remembered that chants are the oldest form of church music, that they were in possession for ages before harmony was introduced at all ; that in countries where their reign has been unbroken they have maintained their unisonous simplicity, grandeur, and *freedom* ; that in England only, and after an almost total collapse of chanting and other church music for a generation, in the seventeenth century, and during its long period of weakly convalescence, they submitted to be brought by degrees under the bondage of (barred) harmony. Harmony, then, magnificent discovery as it was—carrying all before it and even sweeping away from the great field of secular music all the old 'Modes' but two, because they would not readily submit to its demands—nevertheless fell back respectfully before the old simple church chant, and, except in modern England, left it untouched, because it recognized its claim to a freedom of utterance which vocal harmony could not follow. The rule, not indeed without exceptions for festal settings, down to the end of the sixteenth century in England also seems to have been unisonous chanting (Heywood).

A further and very practically conclusive reason against vocal harmony in chanting is that it is incompatible with antiphonal chanting of any kind, except in those few churches where the choir can always muster a full and equal complement of all parts on both sides.

Is it then unreasonable—with the whole of the rest of the Prayer Book open to harmony—to ask exemption for the Psalms, and for the Canticles when chanted ?

But an objection has been raised which we cannot justly pass over. It is pleaded with some reason that with unisonous singing, if prolonged through several Psalms, with a mixed choir of men and boys, even with a limited range of reciting notes[1], the strain is too great for the basses, and will injure their voices. This would in some choirs be a strong plea, but it must be observed that unison is not *forced* upon these low voices in this Psalter, but is treated only as the rule for the choir and congregation in general. The basses can be provided with copies of the organ edition, and sing their part from that; but only on condition that they can and will, as they easily may, adapt themselves to the free rhythm, and not drag back the chanting into the old rigid metrical groove in order to enable them to keep together without trouble.

It will be seen presently that vocal harmony in chanting is chargeable with a further mischief still (see p. 15, note).

If the reader is still unconscious of the wrong done to the Psalms by the prevailing manner of English chanting; if he is still unwilling to face the sacrifice of some popular and musically beautiful strains and of vocal harmony (in chanting only); if he cannot face the passing trouble of overcoming old habits; if he loves too well the easy mechanical guidance of measured music; or if, finally, he rejects anything that is, or appears to be, new; — he will probably not proceed to learn from the following sections the aids that are offered in this Psalter to a more reasonable, intelligent, and devout use of the Psalms in public worship. Only let him allow that the fault is not in the method, but in the critic.

PART II.

Application of these Principles.

1. **Pointing and Accentuation.**—We have now to consider the application of the principles hitherto advanced to particulars; and, first, to pointing.

I. POINTING is the adjustment of the *accented* notes of a chant (which are fixed as to their position) to the *accented* syllables of

---

[1] With the one exception of Sir H. Oakeley's fine chant assigned to the Benedicite, where the recitation is very short, there is no reciting note in this Psalter above C.

the Psalm-verse, which are not so fixed; hence the difficulty of it. And this difficulty is greater in English than in Latin or other languages, because of our 'sledge-hammer' accentuation, as foreigners call it, which renders the suppression of an awkwardly placed strong syllable, or the shifting of the accent, nearly impossible; whereas in Latin, where accentuation is so much lighter and more diffused, it is not difficult to pass over and ignore accents, and to point syllabically, as is constantly done, and as some have advocated our doing even in English, . where, however, it is ruinous to the sense.

Accents to be reduced in number or relative force.—It is then evident that the fewer the strong accents, the less will be the difficulty of adjusting them to the right syllables; because the fewer will be the strong syllables required to bear them. In a word, the less pointing the better. And in this Psalter, taking seven Psalms at hazard, the average number of syllables that are brought under the melody, as distinguished from the reciting-note, is $5\frac{2}{3}$—whereas in the same Psalms in the 'Cathedral Psalter' the average (*without* reckoning their quasi-bar at the close of the monotone) is $9\frac{1}{4}$.

But to understand the bearing of this we must understand the true accentuation of an Anglican chant and the true relation of its parts.

2. THE ACCENTUATION AND PARTITION OF A CHANT.—It has been hitherto generally supposed, as we have said above, that an Anglican chant is by nature and necessity a metrical tune, consisting of seven bars, with five strong and nearly equal fixed accents, two in the first half and three in the second; and as such it has been written and used, thus:—

Example 1.

and the slight inequality which will always be felt in the accents of alternate bars is made, or allowed, to favour the first, third, and fifth; the choir being allowed to gather themselves together after the recitation and come down heavily upon the first note of each inflexion, Nos. 1 and 3, and so of course upon No. 5 also with the well-known 'thump.'

In reality a chant should be considered as in $\frac{4}{4}$ time (*if any*), the chief weight falling upon the second and fourth accents as numbered above, and very little upon the three others. If we allow ourselves, for the sake of illustration, to use bars and to represent the reciting-note, as is often (wrongly) done, by a semibreve only, it would appear thus:—

Example 2.

But the first and third of these accents do not really in singing fall upon any fixed note (or, rather, syllable) but upon some repetition of the reciting-note somewhere near the end of the recitation, and may be well shown thus:—

Example 3.

And this is the way in which a chant should be 'played over,' that is, played without the guidance of words.

But the best way is to consider the chant as having practically only *two* fixed rhythmical accents, and *no* bars, thus:—

Example 4.

'It is incontestible,' says the Rev. C. A. Stevens (quoted by Mr. Heywood), 'that this ought to be regarded as the normal form of the Anglican chant.' (*Remarks on Reform of Cathedral Music.*)

NOTE.—It has been pointed out by Mr. Heywood, that the unfortunate departure from this original form was chiefly due to the introduction of harmony in chants. 'As the penultimate note was originally written as a semibreve, composers of harmonies seem to have been unable to resist the temptation to write two notes against it in the upper parts in order to get the pleasing effect of a discord by suspension, and later in the bass also, from which additional variety was obtained by change of root in the harmony.' And eventually in new chants the semibreve of the melody itself came to take the form of two different minims, with the effect of throwing all the accent on to the first, and consequently inducing a fixed accent on the final note; though for a century after this chants were still written and printed and the words assigned upon the old true supposition that the penultimate was one semibreve, and that the last note should not, and would not be accented, unless the words required it. The Cathedral system of pointing is a modern innovation, arising from a supposed necessity of adapting itself to this deform ' of the earlier English chant.

Again, heretofore the chant has been considered to consist (in each half) of (1) a monotonic recitation, and (2) a mediation of three notes, or a cadence of five (as in Ex. 1, above). Here it is treated as consisting in each half (1) of a recitation partly monotonic and partly inflected ; and (2) a mediation of one (or two), or a cadence of two, notes only ; that is to say, the other two notes immediately following the 'monotone' are reckoned as being properly part of the recitation, of which they are an 'inflexion,' leading it to the climax or accented note of the true mediation and cadence, and not as belonging to these latter, thus :—

Example 5.

(Monotonic) (Inflected)   (Monotonic) (Inflected)

Recitation.   Mediation.   Recitation.   Cadence.

This combination of these two notes with the monotone as an integral part of the recitation of course demands a melody flowing smoothly from the one to the other without wide rising intervals or 'zigzags,' but it demands also, in singing, the suppression to the utmost of the habit of pausing between them, as if at this point 'a tune strikes up'; and above all the suppression, as far as possible, of the accent on the first of these two notes, as it is not the first in a bar.

It will be now understood how the strong accents are reduced in number, but somewhat increased in *relative* force; how the pointing is thereby simplified, and more freedom of rhythm gained. It should also be understood that the actual process of pointing which we follow is, in one important respect, just the reverse of that usually followed. Under both the systems hitherto prevailing the workers, starting as it has been already said, from the idea of a strict metrical tune with five fixed accents of nearly equal force, and seeking to supply a strong syllable for every accented note, work back from the final strong syllable in each half, as far as they find necessary, in order to enclose and appropriate sufficient of these strong syllables, which, falling as they do at very irregular intervals, bring in with them a varying number of others, which have to be crowded into the fixed bars ; the monotonic recitation being considered as merely the residue. The evils of this method are many ; for, to repeat briefly, (1) it depreciates the importance of the recitation in favour of the 'melody'; (2) it encourages a slipshod, hurried recitation, as only a preparation for a metrical tune 'striking up' after a pause at the end of it; (3) it increases greatly the difficulties of pointing ; (4) it produces (in the Cathedral system) a painful crowding of syllables on the last note ; and (5) it involves a number of jingling dactyls and anapaests [1].

The system here adopted starts from the opposite theory, that the recitation is the important part of the chant, and demands the first attention and the least interference. It is held that the melody, having encroached upon it, must be made to recede to its proper position, *without, however, at all altering or curtailing the existing melody, as will be explained.*

2. **The Inflexions or Melody.**—The encroachment of the melody upon the monotonic recitation is twofold. The melody has been allowed to appropriate more than its due share of words or syllables, and has thus trespassed upon the *length* of the free recitation, the essential part of the chant ; and the strong accent which it has been allowed to claim for its first note has given it that separate and prominent character as

---

[1] Not such as are caused by a minim and two differing crotchets in a bar of the *music* (already noticed above, p. 6, III), but such as are due to the assignment of three syllables of the *words* to two minims, which are thereby broken up into crotchets, with the same bad effect. The following happen to afford examples, in each case, of either kind, both of dactyls and anapaests :—

```
 . . . . Lord, | Thōse . shǎll ǐn | hĕr - ǐt . thē | land.
 . . . wherein | wē  hǎve ⌣— | sŭffĕrĕd . ǎd | versity.
```

```
 . . . put | tǒ  ǎ  pĕr | pĕt . ǔǎl | shame.
 . . . . one | chǒ ⌣— sĕn ! out . of the | people.
```

a distinct 'tune' which has so overshadowed the *importance* of the recitation, of which it is rightly but the inflexion and close. Both these wrongs are righted by one means, the free use of diaeresis, by which the two first notes are allowed to occupy one syllable only, as a rule, while by the same means the accent of the first is dissipated. Moreover, the difficulty of pointing is greatly reduced by the reduction of the number of syllables to be pointed[1].

3. **Diaeresis explained.**—It will be necessary here to explain the action of diaeresis, or the assigning of two notes, slurred, to one syllable, e.g.:—

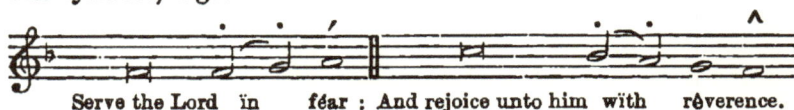

Serve the Lord in féar : And rejoice unto him with réverence.

At first sight it might be thought that this must give additional weight and emphasis to this syllable, which is more often than not a weak one; but the effect is exactly the reverse. The emphasis of the syllable, even if a strong one, and the accent of the (first) note are both reduced. And the reason is this: you *cannot* emphasize an unfinished, and therefore unmeaning, word or syllable, except when it ends with a long open vowel, which is not common in English, and then only imperfectly; and without emphasis on the syllable you cannot, or at least will not, get much accent on the note. By emphasis I mean the accentuation of meaning, by accent the accentuation of sound, musical or other.

There is nothing new in the use of diaeresis, or slurring; it is used more or less freely in all pointed Psalters—but whereas in those it is never used if two separate syllables can be had, here, on the contrary, two separate syllables are never used in this place if it can be avoided.

NOTE.—The only necessary exceptions to the use of diaeresis are the very rare cases in which it would fall on a very weak

---

[1] The terms *Diaeresis* for the *division* of one syllable between two minims, and *Synthesis* for the converse, i.e. the coupling of two syllables under one minim, seem to have been first applied to pointing for chants by the late Rev. H. E. Havergal, in a Paper on the subject about thirty years ago. With Synthesis we have no concern; it is the cause, when used, of the jingling, tripping, effect of dactyls or anapaests of which we have just spoken.

syllable preceded by two other equally weak syllables, e.g. we must point thus, 'honourâblê,' 'adversâries,' not 'honourablê,' 'adversaries'; and two or three words peculiar in themselves or in their relation to others, viz. 'Isrâél '; and the ' Hôlý,' not ' Hol̈ÿ' in the *Gloria Patri*, where it is not a mere epithet but part of a Proper Name ; and 'Sabâoth' in the *Te Deum*, the first ' a ' in which represents no real vowel sound at all in the Hebrew (' Ts'bâoth ') and being therefore unable to bear diaeresis must be pointed 'ôf Sâbâ-oth,' and not 'Sâbâoth' and certainly not ' Sâb·âyoth ' as it is generally, but incorrectly and most unpleasingly pronounced.

No doubt the use of diaeresis with any light syllable, will at first fail to commend itself to many ; but a little consideration and use will remove all misgiving. We must consider that diaeresis was and is still used far more promiscuously and to a greater extent than this in the neumas of the old Plainsong with any syllable of the long Latin words, although the accent is far weaker than our English accent; and that the monosyllables which are far more numerous in English, which is a grammatically non-inflected language, are far better able to bear diaeresis.

It will be evident, also, that by thus using for these two notes only one syllable (the last syllable before the true mediation or cadence), there are left so many the more syllables or words to the monotone, which is the essential element of a chant, while it relaxes the rigid fetters of bars and musical accents upon the free rhythm of the Psalm-verse. There is, moreover, another very important value in diaeresis which will be explained further on.

4. **The Accentuation of the Mediation and the Cadence.—** We come lastly to the concentration of accent upon the final note of the mediation and upon the penultimate note of the cadence, and especially upon this latter, which shall be first considered.

No one who has any experience of both Anglican and Gregorian chants can fail to notice how much more heavy is the accent falling upon the last note of all in the Anglicans. The reason of this is, in part the modern perfect cadence, in part the use of harmony ; and it has generally been felt that this final accent of the Anglican chant, *as usually sung*, is too heavy to be allowed to fall on a light final syllable, e. g. 'salva*tion*,' 'peo*ple*,' as it may be with Gregorians ; and consequently, pointers of the Cathedral school have thought it necessary to go back, as stated above, sometimes as far as the fourth syllable from the end, to find one strong enough to bear it, and then to crowd together on the same note this and all the subsequent light syllables, with a very bad effect, e.g. with two syllables (commonly called 'the double knock'):—

.... gener | átion.
.... to an | óther.

Or with the 'clatter' or 'unmelodious huddling' (Jebb) of three syllables:—

.... shall | pérish | èver | lástingly.
.... per | fórmed | ìn Je | rúsalem.

Or even with four:—

.. bĕ		cáuse it		ís so		cómfortable.	
.. my		hánd a		gáinst their		ádversaries.	*Cathedral*
.. his		cóvenant		ánd his		téstimonies.	*Psalter.*
.. ac		córding		tó our		wíckednesses.	
—		ánd		nót to		cóvetousness. —*Mercer.*	
.. the		ángel of the		Lórd		scáttering them.—*Hullah.*	

The representatives of the so-called 'Church' system adopt a halfway position, and attempt to evade the difficulty by simply ignoring it, and assigning without hesitation to any final syllable, however weak, this final note, trusting to its being sung lightly, which is not, indeed, impossible, but in practice seldom attainable, thus :—

because it | is so | comfort·a | ble.
.... our | wicked | nĕss | es.

But so long as they still accept the old conception of a metrical tune of seven bars, and retain the old accentuation, and still use the unmanageable chants with broken penultimates, it will be in the long run practically impossible to withhold the heavy accent on the final note, and to escape the charge of singing in spite of themselves—|ba-a | túl.—|ri-ich | ées.—|pe-eo | púl.— or, | testimo | nées. Even Gregorian (English) Psalters are infected with most of these faults. It can now be understood what was meant by the statement at the beginning that the 'Cathedral' and 'Church' systems were but one system followed in different degrees, or differing by only one degree.

5. **The unbroken Penultimate.**—With an unbroken and strongly accentuated penultimate, however, i. e. a semibreve, the difficulty disappears, because *all accent is relative or comparative*; the more you accent any one syllable, the less you will and must accent the syllable on either side of it, and vice versa ; and

upon an unbroken penultimate you can concentrate a strong accent, and thereby at once lighten the accent on the final, and make it light enough for a light final syllable, e. g. :—

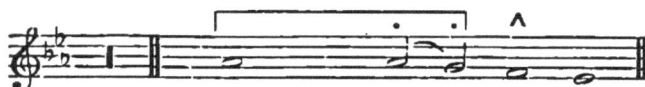

```
. . . generation to  ún  -  -  óth - er
. . . shall perish    evër  -  låsting - ly
O Thou Holy One       öf        Ís - raèl
. according to        öur  —  wíckednesses.
```

This is the method here followed ; and, for this purpose, only such chants are selected as have an unbroken penultimate (see p. 28 infra).

And this concentration of accent on the penultimate leads to another important point. Not only does it *produce* the desired effect of reducing the heavy final accent which follows it, but, conversely, it *requires*, in order to its own maintenance (on the principle just explained), that the accent next *before* it should be reduced as far as possible ; in other words, that there should be no marked accent on the '*inflexion*,' to break its continuity with the monotone. And this applies equally to the first half of the chant, where the strong accent is to be concentrated on the one accented note of the mediation, and drawn away from the inflexion.

6. Occasional Diaeresis of Final Syllables.—There are some few verse-endings which demand a special treatment, which we may call 'Final Diaeresis.'

(i) In those very few cases where there are not sufficient words to supply syllables for all three parts of the second half of a chant (monotone, inflexion, and cadence), without stretching a syllable over two notes, the usual awkward device is to borrow a syllable, or rather a part of it, from the recitation, by stretching it across the 'bar,' from an unaccented note over to an accented note, thus :—

1. ‖ in ⌒| — a | strange | land (= i-⌒| ·in a | . . .).

2. ‖ shall ⌒| —⌒— | never | fall (= sha-⌒| -a-all | . . .).

3. ‖ 'There ⌒| — is | no | God' (= The-⌒| -ere is | . . .)

4. ‖ Worms ⌒| — and | feathered fôwls (= Wor-⌒| -orms and | . . .).

Instead of this, in this Psalter the *last* syllable of the *verse* is allowed to stretch itself over the two final notes, of which the first, and not the second, is accented ; thus :—

```
    1. . . . . ǁ   In a    strănge   lånd  —.
    2. . . . . ǁ   shall   nevër     fåll  —.
```

But the use of ordinary diaeresis in the preceding inflexion often obviates this need ; thus :—

3. 'There | ĭs | nô God.'
4. Worms | ănd | féathered fôwls.

When the necessity for it does occur, it produces no difficulty to the singer, because, having got as far as this point, it is impossible to do other than sing the last word rightly. The greater number of these cases are due to mistakes in the Prayer Book division and grouping of verses, and are most satisfactorily met by correcting this ; and in this Psalter these verses, and a few others where it is necessary for antiphonal reasons, to be explained presently, are given (as alternatives only) in a corrected form ; but, as this may be thought by some inadmissible, every such verse is given in its usual form also, and the difficulty dealt with as above.

(ii) The other cases (not so rare) which demand this form of diaeresis are those where the *last* syllable being a strong one, and *both* those preceding it too weak to bear the heavy pen-. ultimate accent, it would otherwise be necessary to go back to the fourth or even fifth syllable and crowd three or four together on the penultimate note, e.g. we should have to point, '. . . bĕ whiter-than snow,' which is bad ; therefore we point, '. . . be whiter thăn snôw —.' *This* use of diaeresis is not new ; it is borrowed from Gregorian Psalters, in which it is used largely.

(iii) There are also a few cases in which this final diaeresis is used to prevent a false, or enforce a true, accent,—as in the *Te Deum*—'dŏ crŷ —,' 'praïse Thêe —.'

7. **The Value of Diaeresis in regard to Emphasis on other Words.**—It is a very important point in favour of the free use of diaeresis, that it enables us to escape all the false emphaŝes

which abound in most Psalters, and are generally tolerated as inevitable, as, for instance, where a prominent accent is allowed to fall upon a preposition (of one syllable) or upon other subordinate particles, e.g. . . . | wíth thanks | giving ;—corners | óf the | earth ;—Harden | nót your | hearts ;—Hard | senten | cés of | old ;—Com | pari | són of Thee ;—glori | óus ap | parel :—with which compare, in this Psalter, *Venite* 2, 4, 8 ; Ps. lxxviii. 2 ; lxxiii. 24 ; and xciii. 1. There are indeed a few instances, where the choice lies only between accenting a merely neutral preposition and accenting a pronoun following it which is clearly non-emphatic. In this case it would be not merely false, but falsifying, to emphasize the pronoun, and the preposition must bear the accent, as it would in reading, in order to take it off the pronoun, e. g. 'O hide not Thy commandments fróm me' : 'All the day long is my study ín it.'

8. A few unavoidable Polysyllabic Endings.—Lastly, there are a few long, unmanageable words at the ends of verses, or at the mediation, which no method of pointing whatever can make quite satisfactory, e.g. 'adversaries, wickednesses, abominable, covetousness, testimonies.' We reject, as the worst of all ways, the so-called 'Cathedral' way of accumulating two or more syllables (with an accent on the first of them) upon the final note, and, as being but little better, the 'Church' way, which throws the strong accent of the penultimate bar on the penultimate syllable, even if it be the weakest. The only admissible course is to make the strong penultimate (unbroken) accent to fall upon the one strong syllable of the word, even though it leave as many as three light syllables to follow, and to allow these to distribute themselves naturally between the penultimate and final notes ; practically they will fall on the final, but, as they are all devoid of accent, they neither throw any upon the final note, nor produce the clatter upon it that the Cathedral system does (see supra, p. 20).

9. The Reciting-note and the Recitation.—Notwithstanding the supreme importance of this, the essential part of chanting, it has been necessary to postpone its consideration, till the inflexions, or melody, had been dealt with and made to retreat, as it were, from the aggressive position which they have hitherto assumed, and to liberate the recitation both from trespass upon its length, and depreciation of its relative value. We must now provide for the proper use of this freedom, i.e. for the substitution of true rhythm for gabble here, as we have, it is hoped, substituted it for rigid metre in the inflexions.

The *Recitation*, we may safely say, has been the least studied, though by far the most difficult, as well as important part of a chant and Psalm-verse. It is always sung *much too fast*, and sometimes without any attention to stops, sometimes with exaggerated observance of all stops equally. No improvement can be expected until we have learned to recite SLOWLY and deliberately, and, of course, reverently and intelligently. 'A good rule is to sing the reciting-note slowly, and the inflexions quickly' (*Elements of Plainsong*, p. 46).

But the difficulty of inducing in concert this reverent and expressive recitation is, no doubt, very great. No system of marks, sufficiently simple to be readily understood and followed in practice, can be also sufficiently elastic and graduated to express, except approximately, the delicate undulations of true rhythm ; yet to obtain any improvement of our present practice some such guidance is necessary [1]. Two marks, and two only, are therefore adopted, the well-known prosodial 'long' or horizontal line over the vowel or vowels of such words as should be more or less prolonged or dwelt upon, but *not sharply accented*, and a dot, or inverted period, where breath may be taken.

In this way it is hoped to break up the recitation into rhythmic undulations, as would be done by a good reader or reciter ; and to prevent the unseemly hurrying to the end of the monotone which is so common.

The ordinary grammatical stops are left, to serve their proper purpose, except the comma *before* a *simple* vocative, which in reading is never observed. By 'a simple vocative' is meant an invocation by name only, which does not introduce any additional thought : e.g. 'O Lord,' 'O Jacob,' are simple ; 'O Lord God of Hosts,' 'O Lord my God,' are complex and equivalent to a parenthesis. And, very rarely, a comma not actually required for grammatical reasons is inserted for the sake of rhythm.

---

[1] This necessity was first urged upon us by Dr. E. T. Watkins, to whose counsel and constant assistance in meeting it a great debt of gratitude is due.

NOTE.—The syllables marked with a 'long' mark thus, ă, are to be sung *slower*, together with the syllables, if any, immediately following before the dotted syllable, but are *not* to be *accented*, nor is any pause to be made *after* them.

At the Mediation the final note and the final word or words are divided by a dotted bar-line and by a dot, respectively—first, to bring all the chants into the form of those which have two different notes here,—secondly, to insure that the first syllable, where there are two, shall have its full length and not be 'chopped.'

Dec. and *Can.* are to be understood in every verse alike.

PSALM II.

1 *Dec.* Whȳ do the heathen so fūriously rāge tŏgéth·er : *Can.* And whȳ do the people imāgine ä váin thìng?

2 The kīngs of the earth stand up, ānd the rulers take coūnsel tŏgéth·er : Agāinst the Lord, and against hìs Än̂ŏinted.

3 'Lēt us break their bōnds äsún·der : Añd cast awāy their cŏrds frôm us.'

4 Hē that dwelleth in heaven·shall lāugh-them tŏ scorn : The Lŏrd shall hāve them in der̂ision.

5 Thēn shall he speak unto them īn hïs wráth : And vēx them in his sōre d'ïspléăsure.

6 'Yēt have I sēt mÿ Kíng : Upōn my holy hīll öf Sîon.'

7 'Ī will preach the law, whereof the Lord hath said un-to me, "Thou ārt mÿ Són : This day have Ī bĕgót·ten-thèe.

8 "Desīre of me, and I shall give thee the heathen·for thīne ïnhéri·tance : Añd the utmost parts of the earth·for thȳ pössèssion.

9 "Thoū shalt bruise them·with a rōd öf í·ron : Añd break them in pieces·like a pōttër's vêssel."'

10 Be wīse now therefore, Ō yë kíngs : Be leārned, ye that are jūdges of thë êarth —.

11 Sērve the Lŏrd ïn féar : Añd rejoice unto Him wïth rêverence.

12 Kiss the Son, lest he be angry, and so ye perish·frōm the rïght wáy : Īf his wrath be kindled, (yea, but a little), blēssed are all they that pūt their trúst·in-hìm.

PSALM CXI.

1 *Dec.* I will give thanks unto the Lord · with mȳ whŏle heart : *Can.* Sēcretly among the faithful, and in the cōngrĕgâtion.

2 The wōrks of the Lŏrd äre grĕat : Sŏught out of all them · that have plēasüre thêrein.

3 His wōrk is worthy to be praised, and hȧd ïn hŏn·our : Añd his righteousness endūreth fŏr êver.

4 The mērciful and gracious Lord · hath sō done his märvellŏus wŏrks : Thãt they ought to be hȧd in rĕmêmbrance.

5 Hē hath given meat unto thēm thät fĕar · him : Hē shall be ever mȋndful of hïs cŏvenant.

6 Hē hath shewed his people · the pōwer-of hïs wŏrks : Thãt he may give them the heritage · of thë hêathen.

7 The wōrks of his hands are vērity änd júdg·ment : Aĺl his commãndments äre trûe —.

8 Thēy stand fast for ēver änd ĕver : Añd are done in trūth änd êquity.

9 He sēnt redemption · unto hïs pĕo·ple : Hē hath commanded · his covenant for ever; holy and rĕverend ïs hís Nàme.

10 The fēar of the Lord is the begȋnning ŏf wís·dom : A gōod understanding have all thēy that do thereafter; the praise of it endūreth fŏr êver.

In the Organ Edition will be found detailed instructions and suggestions for the effective use of its methods, its notation, and its pointing; and the Choir Edition is prefaced with the directions necessary for the understanding of the typographic marks used, both in the words and in the music.

PART III.

Some Supplementary Aids to Rhythmic Freedom and Elasticity.

The chief means to this have been already fully explained ; they are (1) the reduction of the number of strong accents, p. 14 ; (2) the reduction of the number of syllables assigned to fixed notes, p. 17 ; (3) the free use of diaeresis, p. 18 ; (4) the selection of such chants as allow of the above three improvements; (5) chanting in unison, p. 11 ; and (6) marking the rhythm of the recitation, p. 24. But the hitherto fixed form and length of each strain of an Anglican chant has been a hindrance to that *elasticity* which is essential to free rhythm, and which must be sought in variety of form, character, and instrumental accompaniment.

Variety.

Ancient Plainsong or Gregorian Chants. — One obvious means of producing this variety is the provision of an ancient, as well as a modern, chant for each Psalm ; not that it is to be supposed for a moment that the two kinds are to be used promiscuously in the same service ; this would be altogether wrong. All the Psalms of one morning or evening must be sung to chants of one period and character.

The reader will, of course, know that the two chief differences between Gregorians and Anglicans are first, in the scales, modes, or tones, in which they are written, the former in eight different scales, the latter in two only, major and minor, say C and A ; and secondly, in their form, length, and rhythm, the Anglican being always in one rigid form with fixed accents, the Gregorian varying considerably in both respects. But it is obvious that no principle forbids new chants being composed, either of Anglican form in the old Plainsong modes, or of Gregorian forms in our modern scales. Thus, among the chants in this Psalter written in the ancient modes, will be found some marked 'modern.' These were written some years ago by Mr. Brown, with no idea of imposing upon any one, but simply as a connecting link between old and new ; as, however, one at least of them was so successful as to impose itself, unknown to the composer, upon three or four learned Church musicians, who unwittingly published it as an *ancient chant*, it is thought necessary to make this disclaimer.

Lovers of the old Plainsong may perhaps object to a selection which excludes so many of the best known ancient chants (as we have excluded many favourite modern chants) namely, all those that have a 'broken penultimate.' They will say truly that the same reason for exclusion does not hold good against these, because the incompleteness of the old cadences does of itself reduce the weight of the final accent. But this is not a Gregorian Psalter, but an Anglican Psalter with such Gregorian alternatives only as can most readily be chanted with our method of Anglican pointing; and as the primary object of this method is to induce, with the least possible difficulty and delay, that improvement in our English chanting which is so much wanted, it was not thought wise to increase the difficulty for the sake of a more complete presentation of Plainsong, at least in the body of the book; and we have been content to provide for an optional use of others with those Psalms to which they are best suited, by putting them in an Appendix, with a reference to them over these Psalms. Nor would it be wise to use these at all, until the choir and congregation have been long habituated to the true rhythm, which is most easily learnt with the others.

> NOTE.—It will not be out of place here to point out one other respect in which the ancient chant with its incomplete cadence has an advantage over the Modern Anglican as a musical expression of the continuous Psalm, especially when long; the perfect cadence of the Modern chant brings every verse to a full musical stop, and, as it has been well said, produces 'a series of short bursts with a sharp pull up at the end of each'; and this ill effect is exaggerated by the very marked melody of many chants, and by the wide interval which in some of them has to be covered in returning from the final note to the first reciting note (e. g. Dupuis in D, Heathcote in B♭, Elvey in D; none of them in this Psalter). And this fault is yet further intensified by the sharply defined and fixed metrical accentuation which it is the object of our method to overcome.

Varied Anglican Forms.—On the other hand some of the elasticity of the old chants has been occasionally introduced in Anglican chants by the adoption of the following new *forms*.

(i) The '*New Form*,' so named by those who have already

adopted it, e. g. in the 'Ancient and Modern Psalter,' having a mediation of two (final) notes, of which the second is omitted if there is no second syllable. This is borrowed from Gregorians.

(ii) *Three-note-inflexion'* chants having three notes (minims) instead of two in the inflexions, but in the second strain only. Many of them were originally written before the use of bars and metrical time came in ; and afterwards were used as having one minim and two crotchets in a bar ; these two crotchets are here printed as minims. The effect is the same as that met with in certain Gregorians (see above, p. 10).

(iii) *'Long form'* chants, with both inflexions prolonged to four notes, or sometimes only the second, and with the same pointing as Gregorians of like form (see Pss. cxiv, cxv).

(iv) *'Short mediation'* chants, of the same form as several ancient chants, are provided as alternatives for the *Venite*, *Te Deum*, *Benedicite*, all the Psalm-canticles, and the lxxviii[th] Psalm.

(v) *'Double'* chants, it will be found, are but few in this Psalter ; not because the Editors feel the objection often raised, that they are of modern and very dubious origin ; but because, first, there are but few in existence, about twenty (of which ten have been written expressly for us), which do not fall under condemnation for one or more of the faults which, upon the principles adopted here, exclude a chant from use. And, secondly, on the other hand, there are still fewer Psalms— fifteen only—which fall into responsive or parallel couplets of whole verses, or double antiphony, a condition obviously essential to fitness for double chants ; and even where we can trace this double parallelism between the pairs of whole verses, there always coexists with it the parallelism between the halves; so that, in singing a double chant antiphonally, it is between the half verses that the change from *Decani* to *Cantoris* must take place, the double chant being nothing more than two chants antiphonal in themselves, musically connected, and more or less responsive also with each other [1].

---

[1] It was hard to take as serious a very 'unhistorical' suggestion, made a few years ago in the Preface to a certain Psalter, that double chants are the only complete chants, single chants being merely half-chants !—in other words, that all Christendom until the last century,

(vi) '*Triple*' *chants*, a form of still more recent origin, are upon the same principle assigned to those six Psalms only, the verses of which fall more or less perfectly into groups of three, Pss. ii, xli, xcvii, xcviii, cxxxvi, and cxlvi.

Both double chants and triple chants are treated as optional alternatives only to the single chants which are provided for every psalm—an option extended, not without misgiving, to six other Psalms where it cannot properly be used, that is, not without ignoring the true antiphony and following the old incorrect verse-division.

Varied Harmonies.—A further recognized source of variety is the provision of variations in the organ-accompaniment to voices chanting a Psalm in unison, in accord with changes in its tone or feeling. In some cases also the chant itself is changed; in others its key only, from major to minor, or vice versa.

PART IV.

The Principle and Practice of ANTIPHONAL CHANTING more fully considered.

The second great object of this Psalter, it will be remembered, is to restore the true responsive recitation of the Psalms and Canticles in its three parallel elements, the versual, the musical, and the choral, response; which has been overlooked and obscured by the prevailing practice, not uncommon even in ancient times, of alternating between the two sides of the choir by *whole* verses, between which there is seldom any responsiveness, rather than by *half* verses, wherein the response is all but universal[1].

and to this day everywhere but in England, has been content with incomplete, unfinished chants, and has, as it were, hopped through all its chanting on one foot!

[1] The indications which some have drawn from ancient writers of occasional whole-verse alternation cannot be taken as conclusive, in face of the fact that the word 'versus' was certainly sometimes used for what we should call a half verse,—and quite correctly so, etymologically.

The Choral Response, i.e. between the two sides of a choir, is already recognized everywhere, if the choir is not too small; and this exception need not be made, if the congregation is also taught, as they should be, to consider themselves in chanting as divided into north and south sides. But it is almost everywhere spoilt by the alternation of whole instead of half verses and chants. The true division is marked here by the words *Decani* and *Cantoris*, printed over the first and second half of each chant respectively.

Where there is any doubt as to which side in any church should be *Decani* and which *Cantoris*, the leading side, that is the *Decani*, should be taken to be that on which the Dean, Rector, or Vicar has his usual place, and it should not depend on the points of the compass. This is the conclusion to which careful inquiry as to all our old cathedrals and collegiate churches very clearly leads.

The Musical Response, i.e. between the two halves of each single chant, is so obvious as to make one wonder that it should have been so long ignored.

It is, indeed, not equally well marked in all chants. In all of them the mere suspension and partial close of the melody at the mediation, and the complete close of it by the cadence is quite sufficient to indicate it; but it is still better expressed in those chants which have a musical 'imitation' or 'inversion' between the two strains[1].

The words *Decani* and *Cantoris* over the staff will recall and enforce the true musical, as they do the choral, response.

The Versual Response, i.e. between the two halves of each single verse, is no less indisputable. Nevertheless it requires now to be recovered and enforced in practice; and this is done here not only by the *Dec.* and *Can.* over the staff *which applies equally to the words*, but also by the second half of the verse, which is the response, being made to commence with a capital letter,

---

[1] There is a very interesting collection of chants, recently published by the Rev. H. J. Poole (Novello), in which all the chants, old and new, are selected or written with special regard to this musical antiphony. It is, however, only a comparatively few of them that conform to those other conditions which we have been constrained to impose upon our choice of chants for this Psalter, and most of these, by the extreme kindness of Mr. Poole, we have been allowed to include in it.

except where, in rare instances, the responsiveness fails. It fails, however, only in five per cent. out of the 2,494 verses of the English Psalter. It constitutes the characteristic, in form, of all Hebrew poetry ; and the rediscovery of it by Bishop Lowth in the last century raised so great an interest that it is surprising that it was not recognized as affecting the manner of chanting. The greatest authority, probably, of our own times, Professor Delitzsch, recognizes it as the 'ground-form' of all the Psalms and the clue to true chanting. It has never been quite · without witnesses to its claims ; for at the Cathedral at Oxford half-verse antiphony has been the regular use beyond the memory of man ; and Mendelssohn in his letters from Rome, 1831, tells us that it was (and probably still is) followed in the Pope's Chapel, whence it had been adopted by Bunsen for the German Chapel also. It has been adopted now for some years at York Minster, and in one of the College chapels at Oxford, and in some parish churches, as well as at some Choral Festivals.

NOTE.—Bunsen's advocacy of antiphony by hemistichs (half verses) provoked the opposition of Mr. Jebb in his 'Choral Responses'; but his objections are stated in four brief assertions, every one of which would be just as true, or more so, if exactly reversed.

Exception has also been taken to the general statement that *half*-verse parallelism is found throughout the Psalter, since some verses contain three or even four members or sentences. But *parallelism* (antiphony, response) of lines (sentences, thoughts) is one thing ; *balance* of the number of such lines, when apportioned to two bodies of singers is another, which is not necessary to the integrity of the former. This is recognized by Delitzsch, Lowth, and other writers.

Occasional instances of Defective Antiphony.—As this versual responsiveness, however, does in our Prayer Book version occasionally fail, or is more or less imperfect, it is necessary to explain how such cases are treated in this Psalter.

There are (i) Cases in which a response existing in the Hebrew is lost or marred in the English, by an error either in separating or in grouping the verses ; or in the division of a verse at the colon ; or by the inversion of the two halves of the verse ;

(ii) Cases, very few in number, where though the Hebrew original or its punctuation as we have it, cannot be claimed in support of a rearrangement, there are obviously good reasons for it ;

(iii) Cases, also very few, in which the antiphony is marred merely by the insertion of a redundant particle, which is here omitted *in the alternative arrangement only*, the omission being marked by a dotted space, so that it can be reinserted if desired ;

(iv) Cases in which, on the contrary, there is an omission in the English version of a small particle necessary to the antiphony (which is here inserted, but always within brackets, to mark its lack of authority and enable it to be omitted). In either of these two last cases the particles omitted or inserted are so light in sound, that their omission or insertion does not affect the rhythm, and is imperceptible, except to those who are themselves singing.

Remedies for these defects. — If the antiphony can be restored by merely redividing or regrouping only, the correct arrangement is given in the left hand of two parallel columns, the use of which is at the option of the authorities of the particular church, who will decide once for all which column is to be followed.

If it cannot be restored without an alteration of the Authorized Version,—which is not permissible (beyond the mere omission or insertion of a particle, which has been already considered),—the defect is indicated by the omission of the capital initial of the second half, and by the direction that the whole verse is to be sung by 'all' together. But in those few cases where there is so far a balance or parallelism of sentences that it is only by reason of their inverted order that the antiphony is lost, the verse is left to be sung antiphonally, the defect being indicated only by the omission of the capital letter.

The defect in this last case is due to the principal, categoric self-sufficing, sentence being put after and made dependent upon the subordinate, hypothetic, adverbial, and incomplete one, as in Pss. xxvii. 2, lxiii. 8, lxxix. 13, cxix. 92. To make true antiphony, the 'Versicle' must of necessity be a complete sentence; but the 'Response' may be only an extension, qualification, or limitation of it.

Some Exceptional Cases.

Certain Psalms peculiar in form.—It has been hitherto the unthoughtful custom to treat all the Psalms alike and all verses alike in chanting, as of one form. The following varieties and peculiarities of form ought to be noticed and recognized.

There are eleven exceptional Psalms ; in nine of which, viz.: xiv, xlii, liii, lxxxiv, xci, cx, cxxii, cxxix, and cxxxiii, the first verse, as it stands in our version, is imperfect in its antiphony, consisting of one sentence only, and seems also more or less detached from the rest of the Psalm, either by a break in the construction, a change of speaker, or other like difference, in such way as to suggest that this initial verse is of the nature of an antiphon (in the old sense of a preliminary announcement of the subject of the Psalm); but as it cannot be treated, for practical and theoretical reasons, as an antiphon would be, with its own music, it is here assigned to the precentor (or some one voice) alone, the whole to be sung to the first half of the chant only, the organ finishing the chant alone as a kind of interlude before the Decani side takes up the second verse (first half) as the real commencement of the Psalm.

The two other exceptional Psalms are the cxxxvi[th] and the cxxxvii[th]. The peculiarity of the cxxxvi[th] Psalm (and also of the *Benedicite*) is that the usual antiphonal response between two cognate sentences gives place to a refrain of one recurrent response to all verses alike. The most fitting treatment of this seems to be to let a small body of voices sing each verse, and the whole body of worshippers the refrain. The smaller body might be the choir alone ; but greater variety is attained by letting the men of the choir and congregation take some of the verses and the boys and female voices take the others, as indicated in the margin,—all joining in every refrain.

The cxxxvii[th] Psalm, 'By the waters of Babylon,' seems to have no real antiphonal character at all, but to be a continuous dirge or outpouring of sad and humiliating memories of captivity and exile. It is noticeable that the old ecclesiastics seem to have felt this, for they assigned it to a chant with no mediation (as in this Psalter), the reciting note of the first half running on unaltered through the second up to the inflexion and cadence, with a very impressively plaintive effect. A well-known Anglican chant has been found in a form exactly corresponding with this, and is assigned to this Psalm, all marks of antiphony being omitted in the words.

The Gloria Patri.—This, too, has been inaccurately treated hitherto. The principle of antiphony compels us to put it into its true responsive form as the two halves of *one* verse *only*— a versicle and its '*answer*'—as it is expressly called in those places in the daily service where it occurs, viz., before the *Venite* and Evening Psalms, and in the Litany ; and it must be *sung* antiphonally like the rest of the Psalm-verses, and not ' full,' but *forte* by each side in its own half verse. (See suggestions and explanations to Choirmasters and Organists.) The Amen alone is to be sung by all together.

Special Chants for the Gloria.—A further suggestion has been recently made from more than one quarter, that, whereas the chants suitably assigned to penitential, mournful, prayerful, and didactic Psalms are often unsatisfactory for the joyous tone of the *Gloria Patri*, a limited number of special alternative chants for the *Gloria* alone should be provided for optional use with the Anglican chants, in keys accordant with them ; and this suggestion has been already adopted by the Rev. H. J. Poole in his 'Antiphonal Chant Book,' and is but one of several points in which we have found ourselves in remarkable accord.

The Amen.—The same principle of antiphony has led to the separate treatment of the *Amen* of the *Gloria*, which as usually sung robs the true response of its own responsive cadence ; for the *Amen* is not a part of this response, but rather the general assent, sung by all together, to the whole preceding act of praise, as it is to all hymns as well as all prayers, from which it is always kept musically distinct. Advantage has also been taken in the Gregorian chants of the additional notes which the *Amen* thus requires, to bring the tone to its proper close, which was anciently done by the antiphon, but now, being left undone unless the organist does it instrumentally, leaves the ear unsatisfied.

The Gloria with a double chant.—Again the true antiphonal pointing of the *Gloria*, making it to be one verse only, renders it necessary, when a double chant is used, to repeat and extend the *Amen* to occupy the two last strains,—unless of course the alternative special Gloria chant (single) is used.

'The Doxologies to the several Books.—But, besides this Christian doxology, whereby we give a Christian sense to each Psalm, each of the five Books, into which the Hebrew Psalter is divided, is closed by a Jewish doxology which is too often unnoticed, because it is printed and numbered in our Prayer-book as if it were a part of the last Psalm of each Book (Pss. xli, lxxii, lxxxix, cvi). It is here, therefore, printed apart from the Psalm, and should be sung with the same chant, whether ordinary or special, and with the same accompaniment, as the *Gloria Patri.* The clth Psalm is itself the Doxology of the last Book and of the whole Psalter.

'Hallelujah.'—There is yet one other minor feature of the original which our Prayer Book (not our Bible) version has missed, viz., the occurrence at the beginning or end or both, of some Psalms, especially in the last Book, of the word ' *Hallelujah.*' It has not been thought necessary or advisable to reinsert this generally, except in the margin; but its omission at the end of the last Psalm of all is not only the loss of the natural ejaculation of completed praise, but it leaves the last verse of the Psalm a mere half-verse, shorn of its responsive complement. Here, therefore, it has been restored to its proper place. The full Hebrew spelling (rather than the imperfect Latin rendering ' *Alleluia,*' found in the Old, but not in the Revised Bible Version) is retained as more genuine, and much more true to the pronunciation both of the aspirate and the open vowels.

The Canticles.

The Gospel Canticles, with the Easter Anthems.—As regards their antiphonal structure, unfortunately none of the three Gospel Canticles, as they stand in the Prayer Book, are printed quite correctly.

The Benedictus in the original Greek is peculiarly complicated and obscure in its form—so much so as to have suggested to the learned Bishop Jebb ('Sacred Literature') that its parts have suffered considerable misplacement by early copyists. Fortunately, however, our translators have unconsciously concealed these faults very happily, and it only needs a little rearrangement of vv. 5-8 to preserve a fair antiphony.

The Magnificat in our version has but one false antiphony, i. e. in the incorrect separation (and consequent subdivision) of the second and third verses.

The Nunc Dimittis, short as it is in the Prayer Book, should be, and is here printed in a shorter form still, of two verses only, as well as in its usual length; not indeed without reluctance, but with no doubt at all of its correctness. Ver. 1 as it stands and is pointed in the Prayer Book version *might* serve as the two responsive halves of a whole verse; but it is not so in the original, and it throws out of order the remaining verses. In the original the clause 'according to thy word' cannot be a response, because it is, as it were, imbedded in the preceding clause,—'Now lettest thou depart thy servant, O Lord, according to thy word, in peace,' which is evidently one sentence, one versicle, to which ver. 2 is the natural response, giving the reason for it,—'For mine eyes have seen thy salvation.' And this second verse *cannot* stand alone, for it is indivisible into versicle and response; nor will it, undivided, serve with any fitness as the versicle to a response in ver. 3; for there is no connexion of idea; whereas ver. 3, which is also indivisible and incapable of standing alone, forms exactly a natural parallel with ver. 4 as its response. The two first verses are concerned with Simeon's personal blessedness; these two last —the third in general, the fourth in particular—with his prophecy of the Catholicity of Redemption. That the last verse *could* be divided and stand alone, is an objection which would apply to numberless unquestioned half-verses which consist of two or more clauses.

It is another common error to set this Canticle to a chant or service of quiet and almost sad tone, and to direct it to be sung softly. This is due, as many inquiries have shown, to a prevalent unfamiliarity with the old terminations in '-est' and '-eth,' leading many to read 'Lord, now lettest thou' as if it were 'Lord, now let thou'—a prayer of one weary of waiting; whereas there is not a word or a thought of prayer in the Canticle, which is nothing but a glad thanksgiving for personal hopes fulfilled, and a joyful prophecy of the enlightening of the whole world.

The Easter Anthems, though not written, like the preceding canticles, as poetry at all, do nevertheless fall into very perfect parallelisms throughout.

The Ecclesiastical Canticles: Te Deum and Benedicite, with Quicunque Vult.—The singing of the *Te Deum laudamus* to a chant has seemed to many to present so many difficulties, as to be hopelessly unsatisfactory, and in many country churches it was for this reason the last of the Canticles to be musically rendered. All this, however, is due simply to the unfortunate mistake (no one knows by whom or when made) in the division or pointing of its verses, as we have it in our Prayer Book, where every verse, except the two last, is really only a half-verse, but having been reckoned as a whole verse, has been cut into two (generally meaningless and often unchantable) quarter-verses. To show this in detail would entail more space than can be given to it here ; and the Editor may perhaps be allowed to refer the reader to a pamphlet written by him some years ago, and obtainable now direct from himself. In this Psalter the verses are restored to their integrity, and all the difficulties both of pointing and antiphony at once disappear ; but, as in all other cases of correction, the Prayer Book version, untouched, is also given, and treated as best it may be, for those who hesitate to accept the proposed alternative.

The Benedicite, which is not cast in the ordinary antiphonal form, though it can be sung to a chant in the way described on p. 34, is also set to a special chant in a shortened form, for which there is good ancient precedent, as well as with the ordinary single and double chant in its full length.

The Psalm Quicunque Vult, commonly called the *Athanasian Creed,* though not a Canticle in the usual sense, may well be considered under the same head as the *Te Deum,* because the lengthiness which is sometimes laid to its charge is due to the same cause and is removable by the same means ; for here we find the same unnecessary multiplication of verses and repetition of the chant through excessive subdivision, which has also destroyed, as in the *Te Deum,* the true antiphony of its structure ; for this, except in the final narrative section, is very evident, and is here restored by the same coupling of the severed verses. The Prayer Book version is, however, set out as well, and pointed as usual.

The Psalm-Canticles: Jubilate, Cantate, and Deus misereatur, with the Venite. — These Psalms are of course all written in the Hebrew antiphonal form, and this is rightly preserved in the *Jubilate* and the *Deus misereatur*: but in the *Venite* (ver. 10) and the *Cantate* (vv. 1, 2) a correction is necessary.

This concludes all the cases which have called for any special treatment or any alternative corrected arrangements. *And let it be especially observed that, wherever the Prayer Book version as it stands affords any fair antiphony, even though it be not the true or proper one, our rule (only broken in one or two very obviously justifiable cases) has been to suggest no variation from it at all; and that no correction whatever is made the use of which is not left quite optional*[1]. Some may perhaps ask whether, if we cannot reduce *all* the Psalm-verses without exception to an antiphonal form, it would not be better to content ourselves with the prevailing custom of alternating by whole verses and whole chants. The reply is simple; the antiphony of whole verses is a far greater and nearly universal failure; and the antiphony of whole chants is absolutely non-existent.

Corrections justified; our English Translators.—Departures, though only optional, from the authorized Prayer Book arrangement of verses, would be more difficult to justify, if the question lay between something which seems to us, however obviously, right, and something which we knew that our forefathers in the sixteenth century consciously and deliberately accepted as right; but there is no indication of any exercise of judgement by them on this subject; and these errors may be taken as errors of inadvertence, and their authority on this point as of little weight, especially when we remember that they were making

---

[1] The new alternative, where it is printed in a parallel column, is put in the left or rather more prominent and direct, column, *not* because it claims better or even equal authority or respect, but for exactly the contrary reason,—because, having to contend against both authority and old association, its own intrinsic merits would be overborne without this slight advantage of position.

their translation for the Bible, without any express regard to singing and evidently without regard to the principle of antiphony, which they violate frequently, for no supposable reason except unconsciousness of its existence, and which was in fact only brought to light two hundred years later by Bishop Lowth.

It is remarkable that they cannot even have paid much respect to the punctuation and arrangement of the Hebrew text, for in not a few instances they have so completely · inverted the order of the two parallel sentences, and in others so disregarded the grammatical relation of the Hebrew words, in translating their sense, as to make it impossible to trace the original antiphony or order in the English version.

The Hebrew Punctuation.—But there is indeed no need for us to attribute any great trustworthiness even to the Hebrew *punctuation* itself ; for even Jewish writers have thrown doubt upon it (Smith's *Dictionary of the Bible*, ' Old Testament ').

Moreover, it is important to remember, when considering those places where the Hebrew pointing itself and our own version in following it, gives an inconsistent division or grouping of verses, that it is not with the Psalmists that we are directly dealing in correcting it, but with the Masoretic Editors of the Hebrew Bible, in the seventh century after Christ at the earliest. It was not till then (at the time when the vowel points were also inserted) that the original text was punctuated and accented, the editors no doubt founding what they did upon tradition, but a tradition attenuated by all the centuries that had then elapsed since the destruction of the Temple and the cessation of the public national Psalmody. There is, too, very good reason to suppose that in this their work they were thinking little, if at all, of the *chanting* of the Psalms, and almost wholly of providing, by accents, stops, and vowels, a guide for public readers in the synagogue—in other words for elocutionary purposes. One strong indication of this is the fact that the titles of the Psalms were accented or punctuated, exactly in the same way as the Psalm-verses which follow. As these titles were very probably read aloud by the reader, this help to the right *reading* of them was natural and necessary ; but as they never could have been sung, it seems clear that these accents and points were probably not meant for *singing*, either in the title or the Psalm itself. The title too is not only pointed and accented, as if it were a verse in itself, but is often so pointed as to make it part of a verse (supposing the pointing to be musical) of which the first verse of the Psalm formed another part !

The Hebrew poets themselves seem now and then to have allowed a certain balance of sound or rhythm alone to satisfy their sense of antiphony in a verse, without the otherwise universal parallelism of thoughts. But these cases are not now in point, for no attempt is made here to improve such verses.

> It is indeed an interesting question, how far the Hebrew poets themselves were conscious of any *rule* of parallelism ; whether it was not merely an innate or instinctive Oriental habit, when their feelings were moved, to intensify and enforce the utterance of them by reiteration in other words, either by way of simple corroboration, or by contrast. Certain it is that the habit extended beyond recognized poetry, as e. g. to prophecy (cp. also Gen. xlix.) and even to didactic writings, especially when it was desired to impress precious truths of wisdom on others, as in the Book of Proverbs. And in these cases it was used with just so much irregularity as we might expect in a merely habitual and unstudied form of expression, not guided by any defined rules like our metres.

PART V.

Aids to the More Intelligent and Devout Singing of the Psalms.

Paragraphs and Guide-Notes.—In the necessarily close attention to matters of detail, more or less technical and formal, for adjusting music to words, there is always serious danger lest the true purpose of it be overlooked, and spiritual worship be hindered rather than helped. And, conversely, a satisfactory musical rendering cannot well be attained without some intelligent conception of the spirit of the words. It has therefore been thought right to provide such simple aids to the understanding and thoughtful use of the Psalms as space will allow, by dividing many of the Psalms into such sections as are suggested by change of subject or aspect, and inserting at the beginning of each paragraph and of every Psalm, guide-notes, very brief, very simple, and readily apprehended, and such as may be read, as it were *currente cantu*, and in connexion, or conca-tenation, not with one another, but with the words of the Psalm itself, and such as may help to make the Psalm an *act of worship*, rather than a subject of study, interest, or meditation only— this task under these conditions has proved by far the hardest of any. Valuable as some existing paragraphic aids are, and especially Bishop Westcott's excellent 'Paragraph Psalter,' they are not calculated to meet these particular conditions and · limited aims; and the interpretations of mediaeval writers are so profoundly and perplexingly mystical, and so infinitely varied and detached as to be unavailable, except in a few instances, chiefly in the Proper Psalms, the appropriation of which to the several Festivals is founded upon this mystical and allegorical sense. In this task the Editor has therefore been compelled very reluctantly to work independently and chiefly upon his own judgement.

There are many other, deeper and more beautiful, meanings to be drawn from the Psalms; these here given are only the simplest; and it is hoped that they may lead worshippers to seek for others, either through their own private meditation, or by the aid of such excellent books as Bishop Westcott's, or of Neale and Littledale's, and Bishop Christopher Wordsworth's Commentaries, *The Plain Commentary, chiefly from the Fathers* (Parker), *The Treasury of the Psalter* (Boston, U.S.A.), *A Handbook of the Psalms*, by E. M. Holmes (Wells), or *Reflexions on Every Verse of the Psalms* (Longmans).

The Glossary.—Intelligent and profitable use of the Psalms is in many places interrupted by the occurrence of words either obscure or obsolete ; and an attempt has been made to meet this difficulty by a sparing use of synonyms in the space at the end of each verse where needed ; experience showing that the eye of the general reader does not pass rapidly to a footnote or even to the margin and back again.

Marks of Quotation.—One of the most common sources of difficulty in the Psalms is a frequent sudden change of speaker, especially when God Himself is represented as intervening. To meet this, use has been freely made of inverted commas, and in many instances the word 'saying' or its equivalent is introduced (as it is in some cases in the Prayer Book Version) but in italics, and of course for the eye only, not for the voice.

Marks of Expression.—It would be unnecessary to call attention to these if it were not that it is a common fault, both in Psalters and Hymn Books, to use them too profusely, with the result of abrupt, unnatural, and trying changes for very brief sentences and even for single words. Our emotions of gladness and sadness, which they are meant to express, do not naturally undergo these rapid and transient variations.

The changes should be broad, not minute and elaborate. The principle that has guided us is this:—A word or a short clause in the course of an act of praise, recalling some lowly humiliation or willing suffering of our Lord, or our own unworthiness, inserted for the very purpose of enhancing our sense of gratitude, *should* not, because naturally it *would* not, alter the attitude of our mind and the tone of our voice ; e. g., the reference in ver. 16 of the *Te Deum* to the condescension of Christ in delivering man, and in the next verse, apparently (not really), to His suffering on His way to open heaven to us all, are integral parts of our offering of joyous thanksgiving in this section of the hymn.

As a rule, therefore, change of expression has not been suggested on account of a merely subsidiary word or indirect clause. The 'expression' follows, without unnecessary interruption, the tone of the main direct sentence or paragraph, whether it be of joy quickened by a brief reference to Christ's self-sacrificing love, or of humble penitence or prayer brightened by a passing thought of God's patience and past mercy.

Thus far, we have considered the Psalm-verse and the Psalm-chant ; it remains now to consider the traditional Plain-chant of the rest of the Daily Service, of the Preces or Responses, and of the monotone (inflected or not),—both in the preparatory part up to the Psalms and in the closing part from the Creed to the Collects and the Intercessory Prayers which follow ; and then to add such practical detailed suggestions as may be useful to Choirmasters[1].

Readers who have themselves attempted the task will sympa

[1] The remainder of the Introduction will be found in the Organ-edition of the Psalter.

thize with the Editor in his fear that, in the multitude of details and the complexity of conditions, errors more in number than he hopes, and difficulties doubtfully solved, will betray themselves to the critic of this Psalter; he can only trust that his motive, a desire to aid in the true rendering of holy words in holy worship, will be accepted in mitigation of judgement, and that no judgement at all will be passed until after a patient, unprejudiced trial, in careful accord with the explanations and instructions.

FRANCIS POTT.

SPELDHURST, *October,* 1896.

AD MAJOREM DEI GLORIAM

.